Ali Berber and the Forty Grains of Salt

A folk tale

By Sheryl Gwyther
Illustrated by Christopher Nielsen

 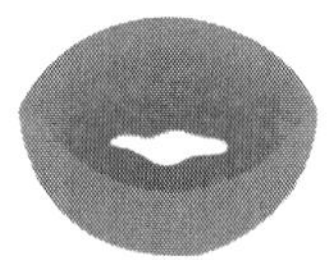 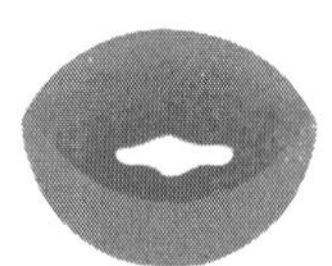

Pearson Australia
(a division of Pearson Australia Group Pty Ltd)
707 Collins Street, Melbourne, Victoria 3008
PO Box 23360, Melbourne, Victoria 8012
www.pearson.com.au

First published 2014 by Pearson Australia
2020 2019 2018 2017
10 9 8 7 6 5 4 3 2 1

Publisher: Dian Faulisi
Project Managers: Tamara Pirois and Rachel Davis
Lead Editor: Kerry Nagle
Editor: Beth Zeme
Cover and series designer: Jenny Grigg
Designers: Jennifer Johnston and Nina Heryanto
Copyright & Pictures Editor: Katy Murenu
Mac Operator: Rob Curulli
Cover art: Christopher Nielsen
Illustrator: Christopher Nielsen
Printed in Australia by the SOS Print + Media Group

ISBN 978 1 4860 0751 6

Pearson Australia Group Pty Ltd ABN 40 004 245 943

Disclaimer
Some of the images used in *Ali Berber and the Forty Grains of Salt* might have associations with deceased Indigenous Australians. Please be aware that these images might cause sadness or distress in Aboriginal or Torres Strait Islander communities.

Contents

Chapter 1	Ali Berber's salty destiny	5
Chapter 2	Princess Portia's favour	14
Chapter 3	A clear problem	25
Chapter 4	A solid solution	32
Chapter 5	A sunny conclusion	40

Chapter 1

Ali Berber's salty destiny

Once, in a faraway land, a young merchant named Ali Berber rode his camel, Sufi, over the final crest of the Atlas mountain range. Ali and Sufi gazed down at the shining city of Alhambro. Ali slid from the kneeling camel's back and patted her curly-haired neck.

A wide grin spread across Ali's face. "That is where our destiny lies, Sufi – in the kingdom of Alhambro. Life will change if my pouch of treasure wins King Aloysius's contest.

We might never again have to trek across the hot desert sands, hauling silken rugs to our finicky, fussy customers. You could spend your days relaxing beneath the date palms, eating as much hay as you like."

The camel blinked her long eyelashes and snorted. It wasn't the first time she had heard that claim.

Ali climbed back in the saddle and Sufi rocked to her feet. Ali's tiny pouch of treasure swung on a cord around his neck. It was a treasure more valuable than jewels, a treasure as pure as the snow on the distant mountain peaks.

They set off down the mountain track towards the kingdom of Alhambro.

At the bottom of the track, Ali saw a notice nailed to a date palm. The words were familiar. Ali had passed the sign many times before.

SPECIAL CONTEST
WIN your WEIGHT in GOLD PIECES!
Issued by
KING ALOYSIUS of ALHAMBRO
Whoever provides the finest seasoning to liven up the king's dishes will win GOLD AND a new home by the lake.

Conditions apply: Anyone who enters this contest and fails will have their head chopped off.

There was something different about this sign, though – a line of tiny words at the bottom. Ali steered Sufi closer and leant down to read them.

Conditions apply: Anyone who enters this contest and fails will have their head chopped off.

Ali gulped and his heart sank. Everyone had heard stories about King Aloysius of Alhambro. It was said he spent all his time preparing dishes and testing new recipes.

It was also said that King Aloysius commanded the kitchen staff like an army officer and did *not* tolerate mistakes.

Everyone also knew that it was the king's daughter, Princess Portia, who carried out her father's royal duties while he occupied the kitchen.

A more alarming rumour was that the king had a nasty temper, and a habit of removing the heads of any who displeased him.

Sufi pulled on the reins; her impatient snort broke into Ali's thoughts.

"I know you are tired and hungry, Sufi. And I know I have not yet won that prize." Ali patted the pouch of treasure around his neck. "But I will. My forty grains of salt are the purest in all the land."

Ali's voice sounded braver than he was feeling. After all, even if his salt *was* the purest, he may not win the prize. His salt must 'liven up the king's dishes' better than the seasoning of every other contestant. But worrying about it wasn't going to help.

Ali squared his shoulders and tugged on Sufi's reins. It was time to face their destiny. Together, Ali and Sufi plodded on towards the shining city of Alhambro.

Ali waited in the Great Hall of the palace, clutching his pouch of salt, while Sufi stood dozing beside him. Ali was suddenly very nervous. Around them, commonfolk, nobles and royal guards assembled among the marble pillars. Ali had never seen so many people in one place.

"How many do you think will compete, Sufi?" Ali asked. "Do you think I'll win? …

Do you think I'll keep my head?" he squeaked. Sufi lazily opened her eyes and shrugged.

"No," said Ali, straightening, "best not to think about that."

With a fanfare of horns and cymbals, the chief noble in the court bowed as King Aloysius and his daughter, Princess Portia, entered the Great Hall.

In a strident voice, the king said to the assembly, "Step forward, all those who wish to enter the contest to provide the finest seasoning to improve my dishes. A word of warning – those who enter and fail *will* lose their heads."

Not wanting to be the first to volunteer, Ali held still. Nobody else stepped forward either. Several commonfolk around him muttered about foolhardy people who were too eager to lose their heads.

King Aloysius frowned. Then he said in a most imperious voice, "Surely there is one brave soul willing to tempt my taste buds?"

Ali took a deep breath and was just about to step out when he felt the full thrust of Sufi's nose. She had pushed Ali forward into the centre of the Great Hall. Ali stumbled and glared at Sufi. Sufi smirked.

Once Ali had righted himself, he took another deep breath and walked with shaking legs across the tiled floor. He stopped in front of King Aloysius and bowed deeply. It was now or never.

Chapter 2

Princess Portia's favour

"I am Ali Berber, a merchant from Randana." His voice shook a little, then grew stronger. "I have brought an ingredient like no other to liven up your dishes, Your Majesty."

Ali held up the pouch of salt and smiled at Princess Portia. He couldn't resist bragging a little: "It is the best flavour this side of the Mediterranean Sea."

"Come closer, young merchant." The king pointed to a small table in front of him. "Show me your seasoning."

Ali noticed how Princess Portia's eyes sparkled with interest as he neared the thrones.

He tipped the forty grains of salt from the pouch onto the table.

The courtiers gasped. The commonfolk jeered. Princess Portia frowned. King Aloysius's eyebrows rose beneath his turban and he glared at the grains of salt. "How dare you insult me with this pitiful display," he shouted. "This is nothing but desert sand.

Guards, throw this fraud in the dungeon. He will meet the fate of all imposters. At dawn, it is off with his head."

Sufi's ears pricked up – now she was paying attention. She scrambled through to the front of the crowd, ready to defend her friend.

"No," shouted Ali as the palace guards jumped to attention, "it's not sand. It's salt, from cliffs beside the Mediterranean Sea."

"*Salt*? What is salt?" asked the king.

"Salt is perfect to add to almost any dish, Your Majesty."

"It looks so ... so colourless … and *small*."

"Your Majesty, I present to you the saltiest salt this side of the Mediterranean. Please, do not judge it by its lack of grandeur."

"Come, Father, surely there is no harm in trying one grain of the merchant's salt," said Princess Portia. She smiled at Ali and nodded her support.

Ali picked up a large grain of salt and offered it to the king.

King Aloysius placed it on his tongue. Immediately, he grimaced and spat it out. "You dare try to trick me with this foul taste?" he yelled. "Bring me water."

A servant ran to the king with a large pitcher, as the guards pushed Ali roughly to his knees.

Fearing for his life, Ali pointed to a nearby sideboard, where a platter of sliced boiled eggs sat, shimmering with an olive oil glaze.

"Your Majesty," he pleaded, "you must try the salt on food. Like on that dish you've so lovingly prepared for your lunch."

Princess Portia nodded. "Father, it is a sensible suggestion." She waved her hand and a servant brought a portion of the food.

Princess Portia crushed several grains of salt over the eggs and gave the food to the king.

The king lifted a spoonful to his mouth, shut his eyes and chewed. Ali held his breath. Not a sound came from the assembled crowd.

When King Aloysius opened his eyes, they glittered with pleasure.

"How extraordinary! That salt added something superbly special to the flavour.

It is beyond my words even to describe."

The king rose to his feet, shook out his royal robes and pointed down to the kneeling Ali.

"I declare the winner of the contest to be, Ali Berber, young merchant from Randana. He wins his weight in gold pieces."

Sufi sighed, relieved, and melted back into the crowd.

Ali beamed as he bowed to King Aloysius, and then to Princess Portia.

All their troubles would disappear now, Ali thought to himself. He and Sufi would no longer need to worry about having enough food or clothing, or about having a roof over their heads. Not that Sufi cared about a roof. Or clothing.

King Aloysius pointed to the remaining salt. "These sparkling grains are as valuable as jewels. Place them in my best, blue ceramic bowls. They will be displayed in this room for all to see their magnificence. Tomorrow, I will use salt in a new recipe." Then he swept from the room.

Princess Portia shook her head at her father's back and sighed. She signalled to the chief noble and said, "Come, we must attend to royal business." Before she left the Great Hall, she called to Ali, "Well done, young merchant. Enjoy your new house by the lake."

The next morning, Ali and Sufi lounged on the verandah of their new home. Ali sipped his glass of sweet orange tea. It had been an unseasonal, humid night but now a cool breeze wafted from the lake.

Even with the damp, oppressive heat of the night, Ali had still had the best sleep of his life. He now owned a real bed with clean sheets that smelled of rose petals. Sufi had her own stable.

And Ali was still to be weighed for his allotted prize of gold pieces. Ali smiled to himself. All was well with the world.

But then, with the tramp of heavy boots and jingle of armour, a division of the king's guards trooped across his verandah.

"Arrest the merchant," yelled the captain of the guard. "He has tricked the king."

Ali and Sufi looked at each other and sighed wearily. "Well, at least we had one night of leisure…" Ali ventured. Sufi snorted.

Chapter 3

A clear problem

Ali and Sufi struggled in the guards' grasp. "I didn't trick the king," Ali cried as they threw him on the floor in front of the two thrones. The king frowned. Princess Portia looked disappointed.

"What say you, young merchant? Did you think you could deceive me and escape with your life?"

Ali shook his head in confusion. "I have done nothing wrong, King Aloysius. I don't understand. What trick do you speak of?"

Ali got to his feet.

"See for yourself!" The king pointed to a table beneath the window where the tiny blue bowls sat.

The guards pushed Ali forward. What he saw made his jaw drop and his heart thump. He imagined his and Sufi's futures and they were not pleasant.

The salt grains had disappeared from the bowls. In their place were small amounts of water.

How could this be? Did someone swap the salt? Ali looked around the assembled court, searching their faces for answers.

"This room has been locked all night. Guards were stationed at the door," roared the king. "What sorcery did you employ to make the salt disappear, merchant?"

"I am telling the truth, Your Majesty. I did not swap the salt with water, nor am I a magician. There must be a logical explanation."

Ali tried to think above the noise of the king's ranting, the guards rattling their scimitars and sabres and the indignant taunts from commonfolk and nobles alike. Sufi looked at Ali hopefully.

"Silence!" shouted Princess Portia. "Let the merchant speak."

The crowd fell silent, and all eyes were on Ali.

Ali scratched his head and thought about the salt. "Magic did not turn it into water," he whispered to Sufi, "so it must be something about the salt itself." Sufi shook her head to say she had no solution to the problem.

A glimmer of an idea formed in Ali's head. The salt came from a very hot, dry place, where the sun and wind parched your throat – a place where there was no water.

Last night had been a particularly steamy, humid night. Could this be a clue? There was only one way he could test his idea.

Ali stood tall in front of King Aloysius. "Please, Your Majesty, I think I know what happened to the salt. All I need is one day to prove it."

The king frowned and pinched his lips tight.

Princess Portia leant over to her father and patted his arm.

"You trust my ability to act on your behalf in royal matters, Father. Will you trust me now? I believe this young merchant. We should let him prove his innocence."

King Aloysius listened to his daughter, and after a moment, he nodded. "So be it."

Ali sighed with relief.

"But!" added the king. "You only have until three hours past noon to prove yourself.

If you fail to change the water back into salt, you and your camel *will* lose your heads."

Ali and Sufi gulped. Ali nodded his thanks. "Your Majesty, I need to take the bowls of water out into the hottest part of the palace courtyard."

The king agreed, and a guard helped Ali carry the bowls into the morning sun.

After the bowls were placed on a wooden bench, the guard tied Ali and Sufi to the heavy bench leg. "Just so you don't run away, young merchant."

A crowd gathered in the courtyard and made loud observations about foolish merchants who tinkered with magic. Sufi glowered at Ali. Ali smiled reassuringly at Sufi and took a deep breath to calm his own fears. Everything depended on his instinct that the salt had changed for a reason.

Ali lifted his face to the sky and felt the sun's warmth. Even this early in the morning, the air shimmered with heat across the city's golden minarets.

"There's no sign of rain, Sufi," Ali said to his companion.

"Thank goodness," he muttered to himself, "because our lives depend on it."

Chapter 4

A solid solution

Eventually, the bored crowd began to count down the hours. After checking the sundial, a man called loudly to Ali and Sufi, "It's four hours before noon!"

"Has the salt returned yet?" yelled another.

"Are you frightened, Ali Berber?"

Ali and Sufi had no choice but to remain beside the bench, doing their best to ignore the crowd's taunts.

"I've never seen a camel lose its head," a child in the crowd whispered loudly. Sufi bleated and leapt to her feet.

"Calm down, Sufi," soothed Ali. "No one's losing their head."

Sometime during the morning, Princess Portia appeared on a balcony overhead. She waved to Ali and Sufi and called encouragement. Ali's heart sang. But when she disappeared inside again, Ali's thoughts strayed to the possibility of an unhappy ending to their story.

By the time the sundial measured two hours before noon, the crowd had begun to disperse until only a scattered few sat in the shade of the palace walls, waiting for something to happen.

Ali sweltered in the heat of the sun and his sandaled toes burned from the heat rising from the courtyard's tiles. He wished he was wearing his turban to protect his head from the sun. His nose had turned the colour of mahogany. By tomorrow, the skin would peel – that is, if his head was still attached to his body tomorrow.

Sufi lay on the ground lifelessly, her tongue hanging limply from her mouth.

They both desperately needed a drink of water.

As Sufi dozed, a slight smile crept across her face. She was dreaming that she and Ali were standing beneath a waterfall.

In Sufi's dream, chilled waters gushed down over their bodies to join the swirl of coolness around their legs. It felt so real that Sufi lifted her head and opened her mouth to drink ... but then she awoke with a start and realised there was nothing there.

"What on earth are you doing?" Ali asked Sufi, looking at her as though she were crazy. Sufi grunted and grouchily turned away.

At noon, with a great weariness of body, Ali pushed to his feet. He glanced at the blue bowls. The drops of water had begun to shrink and at the edge of each was a crinkle of white. Hope rose in his heart.

"Look, Sufi! It might be salt!" said Ali. But with his hands tied behind his back and his legs tied to the bench, there was no way of testing it. Sufi groaned without even opening her eyes.

A servant ran out from the shadows, a small gourd in his hand.

"I come with the princess's compliments. Quickly, merchant! Drink before the guards see." He held up the gourd.

Sweet water slid down Ali's throat – a small amount. The servant held out the gourd for Sufi, too. They both sighed with satisfied relief as the princess's servant disappeared into the castle.

At two hours past noon, the water in the bowls had evaporated even more. Each drop was an ever-increasing circle of sparkling white. Ali couldn't touch it, taste it, smell it or feel it and a tiny, nagging doubt formed that this was not truly salt. But, as the minutes ticked by, Ali's heart beat with excitement. The water had disappeared and in its place, a white substance had formed. Was it salt crystals?

As the minutes ticked down towards Ali and Sufi's destiny, onlookers trickled back into the courtyard, keen to see what would become of the merchant and his camel.

At three hours past noon, the trumpets sounded. The crowd had swelled and become lively once more, watching on eagerly. Ali sat as straight and tall as he could beside the bench, his nose and cheeks bearing the mark of the sun. Sufi knelt beside him, a little more hunched and dejected.

Above the courtyard, the curtains parted on the royal balcony. King Aloysius, Princess Portia and the court's nobles took their seats.

Ali gazed up at them and waited.

Chapter 5

A sunny conclusion

"So, Ali Berber, young merchant from Randana, did you solve the mystery of the disappearing salt?" asked King Aloysius. "Remember, you are on trial here. Fail and you will lose your head."

Ali smiled up at Princess Portia, and then nodded. "I did solve the mystery, Your Majesty. It was as simple as ... as ... riding a camel." Sufi frowned at him sideways. "I had guessed the answer earlier, but I thought it best to prove beyond question that I was correct – which I was."

King Aloysius raised his eyebrows at Ali's cheeky answer. The princess giggled behind her hand. Sufi rolled her eyes.

"So *where* is my salt?" Impatience edged the king's voice.

Ali said, "Untie me and I will bring you the results of my experiment."

King Aloysius jumped to his feet. "Do not bargain with me, young man!" he thundered.

"Sorry, Your Majesty. I'm a little delirious from the sun. May we meet in the Great Hall, if it pleases your royal self?"

King Aloysius considered Ali's words. Then he nodded. "Yes, let us continue this conversation there."

In the coolness of the Great Hall, Ali once again stood in front of King Aloysius and Princess Portia. He bowed deeply, then pointed to the bowls laid out on the table.

"Your Majesty, see how the light sparkles on crystals of salt. They are back, as pure as they ever were. Please, taste." Ali presented one of the bowls to the king.

King Aloysius crunched a salt crystal and pulled a face. He waved for water and drank several mouthfuls. Then he said, "You are right, Ali Berber. Your salt has returned and it's as salty as before. How did you bring it back?"

"I did not do it, Your Majesty. It was the salt itself. It reacted to the humidity last night. When all that moist, humid air came through the window, the salt absorbed the moisture from the air and became liquid. Salty liquid."

"The sun!" Princess Portia laughed. "That's why you wanted to stand the bowls in the sun during the hottest part of the day – to dry out the moisture and allow the salt to be itself again."

Ali nodded, a dopey grin on his face. He didn't have any words to add owing to the distraction of the princess's silvery laugh. Sufi rolled her eyes again.

King Aloysius got to his feet and held out his arms. "This day, I declare a winner for my contest … again. He has found the finest seasoning of all for my royal dishes – Ali Berber from Randana and his amazing forty, or should that be …" the king paused as he made a quick calculation "… thirty-five, grains of salt."

The assembled nobles and commonfolk cheered and clapped. Princess Portia's face beamed with a wide smile. Ali bowed. Sufi didn't know what to do, so she bowed too.

The king continued. "I hereby grant you your prize, Ali Berber. You will be weighed and issued with your gold pieces. Then you may return to your new house."

Ali grinned. They would be swimming in gold and need never again cross the deserts and mountains, burdened with silken rugs for fussy, finicky customers.

Ali and Sufi turned to leave.

"Wait! I haven't finished, Ali Berber," said King Aloysius. "I hereby bestow upon you a new title, the Alhambro Royal Supplier of Salt. For there will be no other in my kingdom who will carry out this task as well as you."

Ali's grin widened even further. He would much prefer to continue to be useful to the kingdom … and to Princess Portia.

Later, Ali rode Sufi back to their new home. Princess Portia and her steed walked beside them. "I have decided something throughout today," she said. "You, Ali Berber, are a very clever young man. In fact, I think you might be as clever as the king's scientists; but don't tell them I said that. It would please me if you were to join my council of advisors … when you are not away travelling to collect salt for my father, that is."

Ali could not have been happier. He jumped down from Sufi's back and bowed before the princess, beaming. "It would be my pleasure, Princess."

Sufi was about to roll her eyes again, but changed her mind. Instead, she stamped her feet with pleasure.

And so, as the stories tell, Ali and the Princess of Alhambro remained friends for the rest of their days, and the young merchant and his camel continued as the king's official suppliers of salt.

To this day, the tastiest salt in all the lands still bears the name of Berber Rock Salt.

The End